PENG

The Penguin Moder ... *ness*
and diversity of co ... *e brings*
t ... *representat* ... *ree poets*
ing, allowin ... *e seasoned lover*
of ... *ry to encounter the most exciting voi* ... *of our moment.*

N JAMIE was born in the west of Scotland in 1962. Her
llections include the selection *Mr and Mrs Scotland are*
ms 1980–1994 (2002); *The Tree House* (2004), winner of
orward Prize and the Scottish Book of the Year Award; *The*
l (2012), which won the Costa Poetry Award; and *The Bonni-*
panie (2015). Her non-fiction books include the highly
Findings and *Sightlines*. She lives with her family in Fife.

TERSON was born in Dundee in 1963. His poetry collections
ber & Faber include *Nil Nil* (1993), *God's Gift to Women* (1997),
g Light (2003), *Rain* (2009) and *40 Sonnets* (2015). He has also
hed translations of Antonio Machado and Rainer Maria Rilke.
etry has won many awards, including the Whitbread Poetry
the Geoffrey Faber Memorial Prize and all three Forward
; he is currently the only poet to have won the T. S. Eliot Prize
. He was awarded the Queen's Gold Medal for Poetry in 2009.

LAIRD, born in County Tyrone in 1975, is a poet, novelist, screen-
r, and former lawyer. His poetry collections, published by Faber &
, are *To A Fault* (2005), *On Purpose* (2007) and *Go Giants* (2013).
w collection, *Glitch*, is forthcoming in 2018. His novels are *Utter'y*
key (2005), *Glover's Mistake* (2009) and *Modern Gods* (2017).
ds for his writing include the Betty Trask prize, the Geoffrey Faber
morial Prize, a Somerset Maugham award, the Aldeburgh Poetry
rize, the Rooney Prize for Irish Literature and a Guggenheim Fellow-
ship. He is currently a writer-in-residence at New York University.

MODERN POETS 4

Other Ways to Leave the Room

Kathleen Jamie

Don Paterson

Nick Laird

PENGUIN BOOKS

PENGUIN BOOKS

UK | USA | Canada | Ireland | Australia
India | New Zealand | South Africa

Penguin Books is part of the Penguin Random House group of companies
whose addresses can be found at global.penguinrandomhouse.com

This collection first published 2017

002

Poems by Kathleen Jamie copyright © Kathleen Jamie, 1982, 1987, 1994, 2002,
    2004, 2012, 2015
Poems by Don Paterson copyright © Don Paterson 1993, 1997, 2003, 2009, 2012, 2015
Poems by Nick Laird copyright © Nick Laird 2005, 2007, 2013, 2017

The moral right of the authors has been asserted

Set in Warnock Pro 9.65/12.75 pt
Typeset by Jouve (UK), Milton Keynes
Printed and bound in Great Britain by Clays Ltd, Elcograf S.p.A.

A CIP catalogue record for this book is available from the British Library

ISBN: 978–0–141–98403–2

www.greenpenguin.co.uk

CONTENTS

KATHLEEN JAMIE

NICK LAIRD

Kathleen Jamie

The Barometer

Last year
Mother threw the barometer
the length of the corridor. This:
she has set her jaw. There's a chill
and the rustle of weeds. She's come in
from the garden, now she'll withdraw.

The maids are shivering. Outside
they're talking of snow. I say no
to a fire – it's an act of surrender.

I can see the bare fields from here
on the balcony. The nights
are growing longer. I know.
At least the harvest is gathered and safe.
– Every thanksgiving
I dance like a Romany. Indian summers;
I giggle and weep. Mother and me
go picnics in the blossoming . . .

My furs are laid out and waiting.
The maids keep tutting.
I catch myself biting
dead skin from my lips.
I have played with my gloves all day.

I ought just to jump
and meet Hades half way.

Julian of Norwich

Everything I do I do for you.
Brute. You inform the dark
inside of stones, the winds draughting in

from this world and that to come,
but never touch me.
You took me on

but dart like a rabbit into holes
from the edges of my sense
when I turn, walk, turn.

*

I am the hermit whom you keep
at the garden's end, but I wander.
I am wandering in your acres

where every step, were I
attuned to sense them,
would crush a thousand flowers.

(Hush, that's not the attitude)
I keep prepared a room and no one comes.
(Love is the attitude)

*

Canary that I am, caged and hung
from the eaves of the world
to trill your praise.

He will not come.
Poor bloodless hands, unclasp.
Stiffened, stone-cold knees, bear me up.

(And yet, and yet, I am suspended
in his joy, huge and helpless
as the harvest moon in a summer sky.)

The Queen of Sheba

Scotland, you have invoked her name
just once too often
in your Presbyterian living rooms.
She's heard, yea
even unto heathenish Arabia
your vixen's bark of poverty, come down
the family like a lang neb, a thrawn streak,
a wally dug you never liked
but can't get shot of.

She's had enough. She's come.
Whit, tae this dump? Yes!
She rides the first camel
of a swaying caravan
from her desert sands
to the peat and bracken
of the Pentland hills
across the fit-ba pitch
to the thin mirage
of the swings and chute; scattered with glass.

Breathe that steamy musk
on the Curriehill Road, not mutton-shanks
boiled for broth, nor the chlorine stink
of the swimming pool where skinny girls
accuse each other of verrucas.
In her bathhouses women bear
warm pot-bellied terracotta pitchers
on their laughing hips.
All that she desires, whatever she asks
she will make the bottled dreams

of your wee lasses
look like *sweeties*.

Spangles scarcely cover
her gorgeous breasts, hanging gardens
jewels, frankincense; more voluptuous
even than Vi-next-door, whose
high-heeled slippers
keeked from dressing gowns
like little hooves, wee tails
of pink fur stuffed in the cleavage of her toes;
more audacious even than Currie Liz
who led the gala floats
through the Wimpey scheme
in a ruby-red Lotus Elan
before the Boys' Brigade band
and the Brownies' borrowed coal-truck;
hair piled like candy-floss;
who lifted like hands from the neat wheel
to tinkle her fingers
at her tricks
      among the Masons and the elders and the police.

The cool black skin
of the Bible couldn't hold her,
nor the atlas green
on the kitchen table,
you stuck with thumbs
and split to fruit hemispheres –
yellow Yemen, Red Sea, *Ethiopia*. Stick in
with the homework and you'll be
cliver like yer faither,
but no too cliver,
no *above yersel*.

See her load those great soft camels
widdershins round the kirk-yaird,
smiling
as she eats
avocados with apostle spoons
she'll teach us how. But first

she wants to strip the willow
she desires the keys
    to the National Library
she is beckoning
    the lasses
    in the awestruck crowd . . .

Yes, we'd like to
    clap the camels,
to smell the spice,
admire her hairy legs and
bonny wicked smile, we want to take
PhDs in Persian, be vice
to her president: we want
to help her
    ask some Difficult Questions

she's shouting for our wisest man
to test her mettle:

    Scour Scotland for a Solomon!

Sure enough, from the back of the crowd
someone growls:
                        whae do you think y'ur?

and a thousand laughing girls and she
draw our hot breath
    and shout:

THE QUEEN OF SHEBA!

Wee Wifey

I have a demon and her name is
                    WEE WIFEY
I caught her in a demon trap – the household of my skull
I pinched her by her heel throughout her wily transformations
until
        she confessed
                        her name indeed to be WEE WIFEY
and she was out to do me ill.

So I made great gestures like Jehovah: dividing
land from sea, sea from sky,
                            my own self from WEE WIFEY
(*There,* she says, *that's tidy!*)

Now I watch her like a dolly
keep an eye,
            and mourn her:
For she and I are angry/cry
                        because we love each other dearly.
It's sad to note
                that without
                    WEE WIFEY
I shall live long and lonely as a tossing cork.

Forget It

History in a new scheme. I stretch
through hip, ribs, oxter, bursting
the cuff of my school shirt, because
this, Mr Hanning, is me.
Sir! Sir! Sir!
– he turns, and I claim
just one of these stories,
razed places, important as castles,
as my own. *Mum!*

We done the slums today!
I bawled from the glass
front door she'd long desired.
What for? bangs the oven shut,
Some history's better forgot.
                              So how come
we remember the years
before we were born? Gutters
still pocked with fifties rain,
trams cruised dim
street-lit afternoons; war
at our backs. The black door
of the close wheezed
till you turned the third stair
then resounded like cannon.
A tower of bannisters. Nana
and me toiled past windows
smeared in blackout, condemned
empty stone. The neighbours had flitted
to council-schemes, or disappeared . . .

Who were the disappeared? Whose
the cut-throat
razor on the mantelpiece, what man's
coat hung thick with town gas, coal
in the lobby press?
                          And I mind
being stood, washed like a dog
with kettle and one cold tap
in a sink plumbed sheer
from the window
to the back midden
as multistoreys rose
across the goods yard,
and shunters clanked
through nights shared
in the kitchen recess bed.

*I dreamed about my sister in America
I doot she's dead.* What rural
feyness this? Another sibling
lost in Atlantic cloud,
a hint of sea in the rain –
the married in England,
the drunken and the mad,
a couple of notes postmarked Canada,
then mist: but this is a past
not yet done, else how come
our parents slam shut, deny
like criminals: *I can't remember, cannae
mind,* then turn at bay: *Why?*

Who wants to know? Stories
spoken through the mouths
of closes: who cares

who trudged those worn stairs,
or played in now-rubbled back greens?
What happened about my granddad? Why
did Agnes go? How come
you don't know

that stories are balm,
ease their own pain, contain
a beginning, a middle –
and ours is a long dreich
now-demolished street. *Forget it!*
Forget them that vanished,
voted with their feet,
away for good
or ill through the black door
even before the great clearance came,
turning tenements outside-in,
exposing gas pipes, hearths
in damaged gables, wallpaper
hanging limp and stained
in the shaming rain.

History, Mr Hanning.
The garden shrank for winter,
and mum stirred our spaghetti hoops
not long before she started back
part-time at Debenhams
to save for Christmas,
the odd wee
luxury, our first
foreign
holiday.

The Bogey-Wife

She hoists her thigh over back fences,
her feet squash
worms, hands stained brown as dung.

She flusters hens, looking for babies:
one eye swivelling in the middle of her forehead,
leaves, like the yeti,
the proof of her footprint.

She's simple, gets tangled in the netting
of raspberry groves; but canny – keeps
to the railway wall, the kitchen-midden.

She can *smell* babies, will push
between laundry hung to dry
arms, strong as plum-boughs
twisting into fruit,

and the old wives run her out of town,
some banging pot-lids as others shout
This is private property! Ye've nae right!

But she is charming when cornered,
speaks a nice Scots,
wears a fresh T-shirt
and attractive batik trousers.

Mr and Mrs Scotland Are Dead

On the civic amenity landfill site,
the coup, the dump beyond the cemetery
and the 30-mile-an-hour sign, her stiff
old ladies' bags, open mouthed, spew
postcards sent from small Scots towns
in 1960: Peebles, Largs, the rock-gardens
of Carnoustie, tinted in the dirt.
Mr and Mrs Scotland, here is the hand you were dealt:
fair but cool, showery but nevertheless,
Jean asks kindly; the lovely scenery;
in careful school-room script –
The Beltane queen was crowned today.
But Mr and Mrs Scotland are dead.

Couldn't he have burned them? Released
in a grey curl of smoke
this pattern for a cable knit? Or this:
tossed between a toppled fridge
and sweet-stinking anorak: *Dictionary for Mothers*
M: – Milk, *the woman who worries . . .;*
And here, Mr Scotland's John Bull Puncture Repair Kit;
those days when he knew intimately
the thin roads of his country, hedgerows
hanged with small black brambles' hearts;
and here, for God's sake, his last few joiners' tools,
SCOTLAND, SCOTLAND, stamped on their tired handles.

Do we take them? Before the bulldozer comes
to make more room, to shove aside
his shaving brush, her button tin.
Do we save this toolbox, these old-fashioned views
addressed, after all, to Mr and Mrs Scotland?

Should we reach and take them? And then?
Forget them, till that person enters
our silent house, begins to open
to the light our kitchen drawers,
and performs for us this perfunctory rite:
the sweeping up, the turning out.

Flower-Sellers, Budapest

In the gardens
of their mild southern crofts, their
end-of-the-line hillside vineyards,
where figs turn blue, and peppers dry
strung from the eaves,
old women move among flowers,
each with a worn knife, a sliver
crooked in the first finger
of her right hand –
each, like her neighbours,
drawing the blade
onto the callus of her thumb,
so flowers, creamy dahlias,
fall into their arms; the stems'
spittle wiped on their pinafores.

Then, when they have enough,
the old women
foregather at the station
to await the slow, busy little train
that will take them to the city,
where families drift between mass
and lunch; and they hunker
at bus depots, termini
scented with chrysanthemums,
to pull from plastic buckets
yellows, spicy russets,
the petally nub of each flower
tight as a bee;
and from their pockets, pink ribbon
strictly for the flowers.

We must buy some,
– though they will soon wither –
from this thin-faced
widow in a headscarf, this mother
perhaps, of married daughters
down at the border –
or *this* old woman, sat
among pigeons and lottery kiosks,
who reaches towards us to proffer
the morning's fresh blooms;
or the woman there who calls 'Flowers!'
in several languages –
one for each invasion:

We must buy some,
because only when the flowers are dispersed
will the old women head for home,
each with their neighbours,
back where they came, with their
empty buckets and thick aprons
on a late morning train.

The Green Woman

Until we're restored to ourselves
by weaning, the skin jade
only where it's hidden
under jewellery, the areolae still tinged,
– there's a word for women like us.

It's suggestive of the lush
ditch, or even an ordeal,
– as though we'd risen,
tied to a ducking-stool,
gasping, weed-smeared, proven.

Frogs

But for her green
palpitating throat, they lay
inert as a stone, the male
fastened like a package
to her back. They became,

as you looked, almost
beautiful, her back
mottled to leafy brown,
his marked with two stripes,
pale as over-wintered grass.

When he bucked, once,
neither so much as blinked;
their oval, gold-lined eyes
held to some bog-dull
imperative. The car

that would smear them
into one – belly
to belly, tongue thrust
utterly into soft brain –
approached and pressed on.

Oh how we press on –
the car and passengers, the slow
creatures of this earth,
the woman by the verge
with her hands cupped.

The Tree House

Hands on a low limb, I braced,
swung my feet loose, hoisted higher,
heard the town clock toll, a car
breenge home from a club
as I stooped inside. Here

I was unseeable. A bletted fruit
hung through tangled branches
just out of reach. Over house roofs:
sullen hills, the firth drained
down to sandbanks: the *Reckit Lady*, the *Shair as Daith*.

I lay to sleep,
beside me neither man
nor child, but a lichened branch
wound through the wooden chamber,
pulling it close; a complicity

like our own, when arm in arm
on the city street, we bemoan
our families, our difficult
cthonic anchorage
in the apple-sweet earth,

without whom we might have lived
the long ebb of our mid-decades
alone in sheds and attic rooms,
awake in the moonlit souterrains
of our own minds; without whom

we might have lived
a hundred other lives,

like taxis strangers hail and hire,
that turn abruptly on the gleaming setts
and head for elsewhere.

Suppose just for the hell of it
we flagged one – what direction would we give?
Would we still be driven here,
our small-town Ithacas, our settlements
hitched tight beside the river

where we're best played out
in gardens of dockens
and lady's mantle, kids' bikes
stranded on the grass;
where we've knocked together

of planks and packing chests
a dwelling of sorts; a gall
we've asked the tree to carry
of its own dead, and every spring
to drape in leaf and blossom, like a pall.

The Cupboard

As for this muckle
wooden cupboard carted hither
years ago, from some disused
branch-line station, the other
side of the hill, that takes up
more room than the rest of us
put together, like a dour
homesick whale, or mute sarcophagus –

why is it at *my* place?
And how did it sidle
through the racked,
too-narrow door, to hunker
below these sagging rafters,
no doubt for evermore?

The Dipper

It was winter, I was freezing,
I'd walked through a forest of firs
when I saw issue out of the waterfall
a solitary bird.

It lit on a damp rock,
and, as water swept stupidly on,
wrung from its own throat
supple, undammable song.

It isn't mine to give.
I can't coax this bird to my hand
that knows the depth of the river
yet sings of it on land.

Five Tay Sonnets

1. OSPREYS

You'll be wondering why you bothered: beating
up from Senegal, just to hit a teuchit storm –
late March blizzards and raw winds – before the tilt

across the A9, to arrive, mere
hours apart, at the self-same riverside

Scots pine, and possess again the sticks and fishbones
of last year's nest: still here, pretty much
like the rest of us – gale-battered, winter-worn,
　　　　half toppled away . . .

So red up your cradle, on the tree-top,
claim your teind from the shining
estates of the firth, or the trout-stocked loch.
What do you care? Either way,
there'll be a few glad whispers round town today:
that's them, baith o' them, they're in.

2. SPRINGS

Full March moon and gale-force easters, the pair of them
sucking and shoving the river
back into its closet in the hills, or trying to. Naturally

the dykes failed, the town's last fishing boat
raved at the pier-head, then went down; diesel-
corrupted water cascaded into front yards, coal holes, garages,

and *there's naethin ye can dae,*
said the old boys, the sages, which may be true; but river –
what have you left us? Evidence of an inner life, secrets
of your estuarine soul hawked halfway

up Shore Street, up East and Mid Shore, and arrayed
in swags all through the swing-park: plastic trash and
   broken reeds,
driftwoof, bust TVs . . .
                      and a salmon,
dead, flung beneath the see-saw, the crows are onto at once.

3. MAY

Again the wild blossom
powering down at dusk, the gean trees
a lather at the hillfoot
                and a blackbird, telling us
what he thinks to it, telling us
                what he thinks . . .
How can we bear it? A fire-streaked sky, a firth
decked in gold, the grey clouds passing
like peasant-folk
                lured away by a prophecy.
                                What can we say
the blackbird's failed
to iterate already? Night calls:
the windows of next-door's glass house
crimson, then go mute

4. EXCAVATION & RECOVERY

Then specialists arrived, in hi-viz jackets and hardhats
who floundered out every low tide
to the log-boat, lodged
in the mud since the Bronze Age. Eventually

it was floated to the slipway, swung high
in front of our eyes: black, dripping, aboriginal
– an axe-hewn hollowed-out oak
              sent to the city on a truck.

What were you to them, river, who hollered
'Shipping water!' or 'Ca' canny lads!' in some now
long-forgotten tongue?

an estuary with a discharge of 160 cubic metres of water per
                                                            second

as per the experts' report?
or Tay/Toi/Taum   – a goddess;
                         the Flowing(?), the Silent One(?).

5. 'DOING AWAY'

Nowhere to go, nowhere I'd rather be
than here, fulfilling my daily rituals.
                                    Why would one want
to absent oneself, when one's commute

is a lonely hillside by-way, high
above the river? Specially when the tide's
way out, leaving the firth
like a lovers' bed with the sheets stripped back

baring its sandbanks, its streamy rivulets,
– the whole thing shining
like an Elfland, and all a mere two fields'
stumbling walk away . . .

Someday I'll pull into a passing-place
a mile from home, and leave the car,

                    when they find it
                              engine thrumming quietly

Moon

Last night, when the moon
slipped into my attic-room
as an oblong of light,
I sensed she'd come to commiserate.

It was August. She travelled
with a small valise
of darkness, and the first few stars
returning to the northern sky,

and my room, it seemed,
had missed her. She pretended
an interest in the bookcase
while other objects

stirred, as in a rockpool,
with unexpected life:
strings of beads in their green bowl gleamed,
the paper-crowded desk;

the books, too, appeared inclined
to open and confess.
Being sure the moon
harboured some intention,

I waited; watched for an age
her cool gaze shift
first toward a flower sketch
pinned on the far wall

then glide to recline
along the pinewood floor
before I'd had enough. *Moon,*
I said, *we're both scarred now.*

Are they quite beyond you,
the simple words of love? Say them.
You are not my mother;
with my mother, I waited unto death.

The Stags

This is the multitude, the beasts
you wanted to show me, drawing me
upstream, all morning up through wind-
scoured heather to the hillcrest.
Below us, in the next glen, is the grave
calm brotherhood, descended
out of winter, out of hunger, kneeling
like the signatories of a covenant;
their weighty, antique-polished antlers
rising above the vegetation
like masts in a harbour, or city spires.
We lie close together, and though the wind
whips away our man-and-woman smell, every
stag-face seems to look toward us, toward,
but not to us: we're held, and hold them,
in civil regard. I suspect you'd
hoped to impress me, to lift to my sight
our shared country, lead me deeper
into what you know, but loath
to cause fear you're already moving
quietly away, sure I'll go with you,
as I would now, almost anywhere.

The Spider

When I appear to you
by dark, descended
not from heaven, but the lowest
branch of the walnut tree
bearing no annunciation,
suspended like a slub
in the air's weave
and you shriek, you shriek
so prettily, I'm reminded
of the birds – don't birds also
cultivate elaborate beauty, devour
what catches their eye?
Hence my night-shift,
my sulphur-and-black-striped
jacket – *poison* – a lie
to cloak me while, exposed,
I squeeze from my own gut
the one material.
             Who tore the night?
Who caused this rupture?
You, staring in horror
– had you never considered
how the world sustains?
The ants by day
clearing, clearing,
the spiders mending endlessly –

Materials

for C. M.

See when it all unravels – the entire project
reduced to threads of moss fleeing a nor'wester;
d'you ever imagine chasing just one strand, letting it lead you
to an unsung cleft in a rock, a place you could take to,
dig yourself in – but what are the chances of that?

                                             Of the birds,
few remain all winter; half a dozen waders
mediate between sea and shore, that space confirmed
– don't laugh – by your own work. Waves boom, off-white
spume-souls twirl out of geos, and look,

blown about the headland: scraps of nylon fishing net. Gannets
– did you know? – pluck such rubbish from the waves, then
    hie awa'
to colonies so raucous and thief-ridden, each nest
winds up swagged to the next . . . Then they're flown, and the
    cliff's left
wearing naught but a shoddy, bird-knitted vest.

And look at us! Out all day and damn all to show for it.
Bird-bones, rope-scraps, a cursory sketch – but a bit o' bruck's
all we need to get us started, all we'll leave behind us when
    we're gone.

from The Bonniest Companie

THE MISSING

When the wee girl toddled round the corner
                                    into our street,
we quit our hidey-seek
and hunkered level with her
oddly drooping eyes. She was no-one's
                        baby sister that we knew.
Was she crying? Maybe. Anyhow
her pants were soaked, so we pulled them off,
left them in the gutter, tugged down her yellow frock,

then gripping a small hand each, me and Sandra McQueen
set off with her,
                    back toward McColl's and the Co-op
– where else could she have wandered from?

Big girls, we knew the way
                        or so we thought
but the road, in its summer haze,
only seemed to lengthen, lengthen, lengthen, the more
   we walked.

WINGS OVER NEW YORK

One of the Central Park
                 red-tailed hawks is
hunched in a leafless maple
pecking at a polythene bag.
When it flies its talons
                 entangle in the plastic
        so it plunges head down
                 – dreadful winged pendulum –
and everyone gasps,
        but with three strong wingbeats
it frees itself and soars
                 (*Where they nestin'?* someone asks,
I heard on Dakota, this year)
above the American Natural History Museum.

At the pondside hop hermit thrush,
fox- and swamp-sparrow
        and elsewhere in the Ramble
sounds a tiny NYPD siren
                 – a starling, high in a red oak.

THE BERRIES

When she came for me
through the ford, came for me
through running water
I was oxter-deep in a bramble-grove
glutting on wild fruit. Soon
we were climbing the same
sour gorge the river fled, fall
by noiseless fall. I mind
a wizened oak
cleaving the rock it grew from,
and once, a raptor's mewl.
Days passed – or what passed for days,
and just as I'd put the whole misadventure
down to something I ate,
she leaped twice, thrice, my sick
head spun, and here we were:
a vast glen ringed by snow-peaks,
sashaying grass, a scented breeze,
and winding its way toward us
that same world-river –
its lush banks grazed by horses, horses
I knew she'd leave me for,
right there, her own kin –
no use my pleas, no use
my stumbling back down
to where the berries grew,
because this is what I wanted,
so all I could do was brace myself
and loosen my grip from her mane.

Glenogil Estate: poisoned buzzard (Carbofuran).

No prosecution.

Millden Estate: poisoned buzzard (Alphachloralose).

No prosecution.

Millden Estate: poisoned golden eagle 'Alma' (Carbofuran).

No prosecution.

Glenogil Estate: poisoned white-tailed eagle '89' (Carbofuran).

No prosecution.

'Nr Noranside': poisoned red kite (Carbofuran).

No prosecution.

Glenogil Estate: poisoned buzzard (Chloralose).

No prosecution.

Glenogil Estate: poisoned pigeon bait (Carbofuran).

No prosecution.

Millden Estate: shot buzzard.

No prosecution.

Rottal & Tarabuckle Estate: dead kestrel
                    inside crow cage trap.   **No prosecution.**

'Nr Bridgend': remains of buzzard
                    found under a rock. Suspicious death.

'Nr Noranside': remains of buzzard
                    found beside pheasant pen. Suspicious death.

Millden Estate: satellite-tagged golden eagle
                    caught in spring trap, then apparently uplifted
                    overnight and dumped on Deeside.

No prosecution.

Glen Esk: Disappearance of sat-tagged red kite.
                    No other transmissions or sightings of bird.

THE STORM

Mind thon wild night
                how the pair of us
got lost, and clung together, stumbled on
                    scared half daft
by a wraith-like moaning through the mirk
till we found the source:
                just a metal gatepost
with a voice the storm had loaned?
– A post we knew: it showed
the path to the croft-house
                   we'd rented cheap
till spring at least, when we went our separate ways.

Mind too what we told each another
                  that far-off day?
Be brave:
by the weird-song in the dark you'll find your way.

SOLSTICE II

Here comes the sun
                   summiting the headland – pow!
straight through the windows of the 10.19
– and here's us passengers,
                splendid and blinking
                      like we're all re-born,
remade exactly, and just where we left off:
the students, the toddler, the tattoo'd lass,
the half dozen roustabouts
                   headed off-shore
                     cracking more beers and more jokes.

Angus at midwinter
                  or near as makes no odds –
fair shadows raxed
over fields of dour earth,

every fairmer's fenceposts
                splashed with gold.

ARBOUR

A sea-side arbour, a garden shanty,
knocked together out of driftwood and furnished
with a beat-up sofa
                    is where I sit,
striving to cultivate the strandline's

take-it-or-leave-it attitude, and happy to remain
till the last young blackbird
                        flies the nest
lodged in the dog-rose to my left.

From time to time father bird
hops across our common square of grass,
                        cocking his head.
Friend, it's the sea you hear, vast and just
beyond those dunes, beyond your blackbird's ken,

but what do I know? May is again pegged out
across the whole northern hemisphere, and today
is my birthday. Sudden hailstones sting
this provisional asylum. We are not done yet.

Don Paterson

The Ferryman's Arms

About to sit down with my half-pint of Guinness
I was magnetized by a remote phosphorescence
and drawn, like a moth, to the darkened back room
where a pool-table hummed to itself in the corner.
With ten minutes to kill and the whole place deserted
I took myself on for the hell of it. Slotting
a coin in the tongue, I looked round for a cue –
while I stood with my back turned, the balls were deposited
with an abrupt intestinal rumble; a striplight
batted awake in its dusty green cowl.
When I set down the cue-ball inside the parched D
it clacked on the slate; the nap was so threadbare
I could screw back the globe, given somewhere to stand.
As physics itself becomes something negotiable
a rash of small miracles covers the shortfall.
I went on to make an immaculate clearance.
A low punch with a wee dab of side, and the black
did the vanishing trick while the white stopped
before gently rolling back as if nothing had happened,
shouldering its way through the unpotted colours.

The boat chugged up the little stone jetty
without breaking the skin of the water, stretching,
as black as my stout, from somewhere unspeakable
to here, where the foaming lip mussitates endlessly,
trying, with a nutter's persistence, to read
and re-read the shoreline. I got aboard early,
remembering the ferry would leave on the hour
even for only my losing opponent;
but I left him there, stuck in his tent of light, sullenly
knocking the balls in, for practice, for next time.

An Elliptical Stylus

My uncle was beaming: 'Aye, yer elliptical stylus –
fairly brings out a' the wee details.'
Balanced at a fraction of an ounce
the fat cartridge sank down like a feather;
music billowed into three dimensions
as if we could have walked between the players.

My Dad, who could appreciate the difference,
went to Largs to buy an elliptical stylus
for our ancient, beat-up Philips turntable.
We had the guy in stitches: 'You can't . . .
Er . . . you'll have to *upgrade your equipment.*'
Still smirking, he sent us from the shop
with a box of needles, thick as carpet-tacks,
the only sort they made to fit our model.

(Supposing I'd been *his* son: let's eavesdrop
on 'Fidelities', the poem I'm writing now:
The day my father died, he showed me how
he'd prime the deck for optimum performance:
it's that lesson I recall – how he'd refine
the arm's weight, to leave the stylus balanced
somewhere between ellipsis and precision,
as I gently lower the sharp nib to the line
and wait for it to pick up the vibration
till it moves across the page, like a cardiograph . . .)

We drove back slowly, as if we had a puncture;
my Dad trying not to blink, and that man's laugh
stuck in my head, which is where the story sticks,
and any attempt to cauterize this fable
with something axiomatic on the nature

of articulacy and inheritance,
since he can well afford to make his *own*
excuses, you your own interpretation.
But if you still insist on resonance –
I'd swing for him, and every other cunt
happy to let my father know his station,
which probably includes yourself. To be blunt.

Poem

after Ladislav Skala

The ship pitched in the rough sea
and I could bear it no longer
so I closed my eyes
and imagined myself on a ship
in a rough sea-crossing.

The woman rose up below me
and I could bear it no longer
so I closed my eyes
and imagined myself making love
to the very same woman.

When I came into the world
I closed my eyes
and imagined my own birth.
Still
I have not opened my eyes to this world.

Bedfellows

An inch or so above the bed
   the yellow blindspot hovers
where the last incumbent's greasy head
   has worn away the flowers.

Every night I have to rest
   my head in his dead halo;
I feel his heart tick in my wrist;
   then, below the pillow,

his suffocated voice resumes
   its dreary innuendo:
there are other ways to leave the room
   than the door and the window

A Private Bottling

'So I will go, then. I would rather grieve over your absence
than over you.'
    – *Antonio Porchia*

Back in the same room that an hour ago
we had led, lamp by lamp, into the darkness
I sit down and turn the radio on low
as the last girl on the planet still awake
reads a dedication to the ships
and puts on a recording of the ocean.

I carefully arrange a chain of nips
in a big fairy-ring; in each square glass
the tincture of a failed geography,
its dwindled burns and woodlands, whin-fires, heather,
the sklent of its wind and salty rain,
the love-worn habits of its working-folk,
the waveform of their speech, and by extension
how they sing, make love, or take a joke.

So I have a good nose for this sort of thing.

Then I will suffer kiss after fierce kiss
letting their gold tongues slide along my tongue
as each gives up, in turn, its little song
of the patient years in glass and sherry-oak,
the shy negotiations with the sea,
air and earth, the trick of how the peat-smoke
was shut inside it, like a black thought.

Tonight I toast her with the extinct malts
of Ardlussa, Ladyburn and Dalintober

and an ancient pledge of passionate indifference:
Ochon o do dhóigh mé mo chlairsach ar a shon,
wishing her health, as I might wish her weather.

When the circle is closed and I have drunk myself sober
I will tilt the blinds a few degrees, and watch
the dawn grown in a glass of liver-salts,
wait for the birds, the milk-float's sweet nothings,
then slip back to the bed where she lies curled,
replace the live egg of her burning ass
gently, in the cold nest of my lap,
as dead to her as she is to the world.

*

Here we are again; it is precisely
twelve, fifteen, thirty years down the road
and one turn higher up the spiral chamber
that separates the burnt ale and dark grains
of what I know, from what I can remember.
Now each glass holds its micro-episode
in permanent suspension, like a movie-frame
on acetate, until it plays again,
revivified by a suave connoisseurship
that deepens in the silence and the dark
to something like an infinite sensitivity.
This is no romantic fantasy: my father
used to know a man who'd taste the sea,
then leave his nets strung out along the bay
because there were no fish in it that day.

Everything is in everything else. It is a matter
of attunement, as once, through the hiss and backwash,
I steered the dial into the voice of God

slightly to the left of Hilversum,
half-drowned by some big, blurry waltz
the way some stars obscure their dwarf companions
for centuries, till someone thinks to look.

In the same way, I can isolate the feints
of feminine effluvia, carrion, shite,
those rogues and toxins only introduced
to give the composition a little weight
as rough harmonics do the violin-note
or Pluto, Cheiron and the lesser saints
might do to our lives, for all you know.
(By Christ, you would recognize their absence
as anyone would testify, having sunk
a glass of *North British*, run off a patent still
in some sleet-hammered satellite of Edinburgh:
a bleak spirit no amount of caramel
could sweeten or disguise, its after-effect
somewhere between a blanket-bath and a sad wank.
There is, no doubt, a bar in Lothian
where it is sworn upon and swallowed neat
by furloughed riggers and the Special Police,
men who hate the company of women.)

O whiskies of Long Island and Provence!
This little number catches at the throat
but is all sweetness in the finish: my tongue trips
first through burning brake-fluid, then nicotine,
pastis, *Diorissimo* and wet grass;
another is silk sleeves and lip-service
with a kick like a smacked puss in a train-station;
another, the light charge and the trace of zinc
tap-water picks up at the moon's eclipse.
You will know the time I mean by this.

Because your singular absence, in your absence,
has bred hard, tonight I take the waters
with the whole clan: our faceless ushers, bridesmaids,
our four Shelties, three now ghosts of ghosts;
our douce sons and our lovely loudmouthed daughters
who will, by this late hour, be fully grown,
perhaps with unborn children of their own.
So, finally, let me propose a toast:
not to love, or life, or real feeling,
but to their sentimental residue;
to your sweet memory, but not to you.

The sun will close its circle in the sky
before I close my own, and drain the purely
offertory glass that tastes of nothing
but silence, burnt dust on the valves, and whisky.

The Lover

after Propertius

Poor mortals, with your horoscopes and blood-tests –
what hope is there for you? Even if the plane
lands you safely, why should you not return
to your home in flames or ruins, your wife absconded,
the children blind and dying in their cots?
Even sitting quiet in a locked room
the perils are infinite and unforeseeable.
Only the lover walks upon the earth
careless of what the fates prepare for him:

so you step out at the lights, almost as if
you half-know that today you are the special one.
The woman in the windshield lifting away
her frozen cry, a white mask on a stick,
reveals herself as grey-eyed Atropos;
the sun leaves like a rocket; the sky goes out;
the road floods and widens; on the distant kerb
the lost souls groan and mew like sad trombones;
the ambulance glides up with its black sail –

when somewhere in the other world, she fills
your name full of her breath again, and at once
you float to your feet: the dark rose on your shirt
folds itself away, and you slip back
into the crowd, who, being merely human,
must remember nothing of this incident.
Just one flea-ridden dog chained to the railings,
who might be Cerberus, or patient Argos,
looks on, knowing the great law you have flouted.

Imperial

Is it normal to get this wet? Baby, I'm frightened –
I covered her mouth with my own;
she lay in my arms till the storm-window brightened
and stood at our heads like a stone

After months of jaw jaw, determined that neither
win ground, or be handed the edge,
we gave ourselves up, one to the other
like prisoners over a bridge

and no trade was ever so fair or so tender;
so where was the flaw in the plan,
the night we lay down on the flag of surrender
and woke on the flag of Japan

Advice

My advice? To watch, and wait for the tide to turn –
wait as the beached boat waits, without a thought
for either its own waiting, or departure.
As I put it so well myself: 'The patient triumph
since life is long, and art merely a toy.'

Well – okay – supposing life is short,
and the sea never touches your little boat –
just wait, and watch, and wait, for art is long;
whatever. To be quite honest with you,
none of this is terribly important.

Sigh

                         Again
                     my heart
                   creaks
              on its hinge
         and with a long
                     sigh
              opens on
         the arcade
                   of my short
                   history
              where
                   the orange
         and acacia
    are flowering
    in the courtyard
                   and the fountain
              sings
                   then speaks
              its love song
              to no one

Waking with Russell

Whatever the difference is, it all began
the day we woke up face-to-face like lovers
and his four-day-old smile dawned on him again,
possessed him, till it would not fall or waver;
and I pitched back not my old hard-pressed grin
but his own smile, or one I'd rediscovered.
Dear son, I was *mezzo del cammin*
and the true path was as lost to me as ever
when you cut in front and lit it as you ran.
See how the true gift never leaves the giver:
returned and redelivered, it rolled on
until the smile poured through us like a river.
How fine, I thought, this waking amongst men!
I kissed your mouth and pledged myself forever.

Letter to the Twins

'. . . for it is said, they went to school at Gabii, and were well instructed in letters, and other accomplishments befitting their birth. And they were called Romulus and Remus (from *ruma*, the dug), as we had before, because they were found sucking the wolf.'

    – *Plutarch*, Parallel Lives

Dear sons – for I am not, as you believed,
your uncle – forgive me now my dereliction.
In those nine months the single thought that grieved
me most was not your terrible instruction

in the works of men, the disillusionments –
Nanking and Srebrenica, Babi Yar –
you, bent above those tables of events
by whose low indices you might infer

how far you'd fallen. No, it was instead
the years you'd spend reconstituting all
the billion tedious skills of humanhood:
the infinite laws of Rome, the protocols

of every minor court and consulate –
the city that must rise up from its razed
foundations, mirrored and immaculate,
for as often as we come back to this place.

In sum, they might account it a disaster
but whatever I did, I did it as a deft
composer of the elements, the master
of all terrestrial drag and spin and heft;

look at this hand – the way it knows how light
to grip the pen, how far above the brim
to fill the cup, or hard to steer the kite,
or slowly it can travel through the flame.

More, it knows the vanity of each.
But were I to commend just one reserve
of study – one I promise that will teach
you nothing of *use*, and so not merely serve

to deepen your attachment or your debt,
where each small talent added to the horde
is doubled in its spending, and somehow yet
no more or less than its own clean reward –

it would be this: the honouring of your lover.
Learn this and she will guide you, if not home
then at least to its true memory. Then wherever
the world loses you, in her you are the same.

First, she will address you in a tongue
so secret she must close her mouth on yours.
In the curves and corners of this silent song
will lie the whole code of your intercourse.

Then, as you break, at once you understand
how the roses of her breast will draw in tight
at your touch, how that parched scrubland
between her thighs breaks open into wet

suddenly, as though you'd found the stream
running through it like a seam of milk;
know, by its tiny pulse and its low gleam
just where the pearl sits knuckled in its silk,

how that ochre-pink anemone relaxes
and unknots under your light hand and white spit;
and how that lovely mouth that has no kiss
will take the deepest you can plant in it;

and how to make that shape that boys, alas,
will know already as the sign for *gun*
yet slide it with a woman's gentleness
till you meet the other muzzle coming down.

Now, in all humility, retrace
your steps, that you might understand in full
the privilege that brought you to this place,
that let you know the break below the wool:

and as you lie there side by side, and feel
the wet snout of her womb nuzzle and lather
your fingertips – then you might recall
your mother; or her who said she was your mother.

The Rat

A young man wrote a poem about a rat.
It was the best poem ever written about a rat.
To read it was to ask the rat to perch
on the arm of your chair until you turned the page.
So we wrote to him, but heard nothing; we called,
and called again; then finally we sailed
to the island where he kept the only shop
and rapped his door until he opened up.

We took away his poems. Our hands shook
with excitement. We read them on lightboxes,
under great lamps. They were not much good.
So we offered what advice we could
on his tropes and turns, his metrical comportment,
on the wedding of the word to the event,
and suggested that he might read this or that.
We said *Now: write us more poems like The Rat.*

All we got was cheek from him. Then silence.
We gave up on him. Him with his green arrogance
and ingratitude and his one lucky strike.
But today I read The Rat again. Its reek
announced it; then I saw its pisshole stare;
line by line it strained into the air.
Then it hissed. *For all the craft and clever-clever*
you did not write me, fool. Nor will you ever.

A Gift

That night she called his name, not mine
    and could not call it back
I shamed myself, and thought of that blind
    girl in Kodiak

who sat out on the stoop each night
    to watch the daylight fade
and lift her child down to the gate
    cut in the palisade

and what old caution love resigned
    when through that misty stare
she passed the boy not to her bearskinned
    husband but the bear

from *Orpheus*

A version of Rilke's Die Sonette an Orpheus

THE DEAD

Our business is with fruit and leaf and bloom.
Though they speak with more than just the season's tongue –
the colours that they blaze from the dark loam
all have something of the jealous tang

of the dead about them. What do we know of their part
in this, those secret brothers of the harrow,
invigorators of the soil – oiling the dirt
so liberally with their essence, their black marrow?

But here's the question: are the flower and fruit
held out to us in love, or merely thrust
up at us, their masters, like a fist?

Or are *they* the lords, asleep amongst the roots,
granting to us in their great largesse
this hybrid thing – part brute force, part mute kiss?

THE BALL

What happened to that little brotherhood,
lords of the scattered gardens of the city?
We were all so shy, I never understood
how we hooked up in the first place; like the lamb

with the scroll that spoke, we too spoke in silence.
It seemed when we were happy it was no one's;
whose ball *was* it? In all the anxiety
of that last summer, it melted in the scrum:

the street leaned like a stage-set, the traffic
rolled around us, like huge toys; nobody
knew us. What was the real in that All?

Nothing. Just the ball. Its glorious arc.
Not even the kids . . . But sometimes one, already
fading, stepped below it as it fell.

THE DRINKING FOUNTAIN

O tireless giver, holy cataract,
conductor of the inexhaustible One –
your clear tongue, lifting through the mask of stone
you hold before your face . . . Behind you, aqueducts

vanish into the distance. From the Apennine
foothills, through the wheat fields and the graveyards,
they bear the sacred utterance, the words
that arrive for ever, blackening your chin

to fall into the basin that lies rapt
to your constant murmur, like a sleeping ear.
Marmoreal circumstance. Listening rock.

An ear of Earth's, so she only really talks
to herself. So when we're filling up our pitcher,
it feels to her that someone interrupts.

THE BEGGAR

Gold lies pampered in its vaults somewhere,
intimate with thousands. But that blind man . . .
like the square of dust below a chair,
a stranger to the very lowest coin.

Gold parades along the High Street shops,
all done up in flowers and silks and furs.
The silent man stands in the silent gaps
between its breathing as it sleeps or stirs.

How does that hand close itself each evening?
Every sunrise, fate sends it abroad –
so frail and luminous, it must amaze

the one who sees it clearly. Let him praise
its dreadful endurance: that only sings
to the singer; that's heard just by the god.

BEING

Silent comrade of the distances,
know that space dilates with your own breath;
ring out, as a bell into the Earth
from the dark rafters of its own high place –

then watch what feeds on you grow strong again.
Learn the transformations through and through:
what in your life has most tormented you?
If the water's sour, turn it into wine.

Our senses cannot fathom this night, so
be the meaning of their strange encounter;
at their crossing, be the radiant centre.

And should the world itself forget your name
say this to this still earth: *I flow.*
Say this to the quick stream: *I am.*

Two Trees

One morning, Don Miguel got out of bed
with one idea rooted in his head:
to graft his orange to his lemon tree.
It took him the whole day to work them free,
lay open their sides, and lash them tight.
For twelve months, from the shame or from the fright
they put forth nothing; but one day there appeared
two lights in the dark leaves. Over the years
the limbs would get themselves so tangled up
each bough looked like it gave a double crop,
and not one kid in the village didn't know
the magic tree in Miguel's patio.

The man who bought the house had had no dream
so who can say what dark malicious whim
led him to take his axe and split the bole
along its fused seam, then dig two holes.
And no, they did not die from solitude;
nor did their branches bear a sterile fruit;
nor did their unhealed flanks weep every spring
for those four yards that lost them everything,
as each strained on its shackled root to face
the other's empty, intricate embrace.
They were trees, and trees don't weep or ache or shout.
And trees are all this poem is about.

Correctives

The shudder in my son's left hand
he cures with one touch from his right,
two fingertips laid feather-light
to still his pen. He understands

the whole man must be his own brother
for no man is himself alone;
though some of us have never known
the one hand's kindness to the other.

The Lie

As was my custom, I'd risen a full hour
before the house had woken to make sure
that everything was in order with The Lie,
his drip changed and his shackles all secure.

I was by then so practised in this chore
I'd counted maybe thirteen years or more
since last I'd felt the urge to meet his eye.
Such, I liked to think, was our rapport.

I was at full stretch to test some ligature
when I must have caught a ragged thread, and tore
his gag away; though as he made no cry,
I kept on with my checking as before.

Why do you call me The Lie? he said. I swore:
it was a child's voice. I looked up from the floor.
The dark had turned his eyes to milk and sky
and his arms and legs were all one scarlet sore.

He was a boy of maybe three or four.
His straps and chains were all the things he wore.
Knowing I could make him no reply
I took the gag before he could say more

and put it back as tight as it would tie
and locked the door and locked the door and locked the door

Song for Natalie 'Tusja' Beridze

O Natalie, O TBA, O Tusja: I had long assumed the terrorist's balaclava that you sport on the cover of *Annulé* –
which was, for too long, the only image of you I possessed –
was there to conceal some ugliness or deformity
or perhaps merely spoke (and here, I hoped against hope) of a young woman struggling
with a crippling shyness. How richly this latter theory has been confirmed by my Googling!

O who is this dark angel with her unruly Slavic eyebrows ranged like two duelling pistols, lightly sweating in the pale light of the TTF screen?
O behold her shaded, infolded concentration, her heartbreakingly beautiful face so clearly betraying the true focus of one not merely content – as, no doubt, were others at the Manöver Elektronische Festival in Wien –
to hit *play* while making some fraudulent correction to a volume slider
but instead deep in the manipulation of some complex real-time software, such as Ableton Live, MAX/MSP or Supercollider.

O Natalie, how can I pay tribute to your infinitely versatile blend of Nancarrow, Mille Plateaux, Venetian Snares, Xenakis, Boards of Canada and Nobukazu Takemura
to say nothing of those radiant pads – so strongly reminiscent of the mid-century bitonal pastoral of Charles Koechlin in their harmonic bravura –
or your fine vocals, which, while admittedly limited in range and force, are nonetheless so much more affecting than the affected Arctic whisperings of those interchangeably dreary

Stinas and Hannes and Björks, being in fact far closer in
spirit to a kind of glitch-hop Blossom Dearie?

I have also deduced from your staggeringly ingenious
employment of some pretty basic wavetables
    that unlike many of your East European counterparts,
all your VST plug-ins, while not perhaps the best
available
    probably have a legitimate upgrade path – indeed I imagine
your entire DAW as pure as the driven snow, and not in any
way buggy or virusy
    which makes me love you more, demonstrating as it does
an excess of virtue given your country's well-known talent
for software piracy.

Though I should confess that at times I find your habit of
maxxing
    the range with those bat-scaring ring-modulated sine-
bursts and the more distressing psychoacoustic properties
of phase inversion in the sub-bass frequencies somewhat
taxing
    you are nonetheless as beautiful as the mighty Boards
themselves in your shameless organicizing of the code,
    as if you had mined those saws and squares and ramps
straight from the Georgian motherlode.

O Natalie – I forgive you everything, even your
catastrophic adaption of those lines from 'Dylan's' already
shite
Do Not Go Gentle Into That Good Night
    in the otherwise magnificent 'Sleepwalkers', and when you
open up those low-
    pass filters in what sounds like a Minimoog emulation they
seem to open in my heart also.

O Natalie: know that I do not, repeat, do *not* imagine you
with a reconditioned laptop bought with a small grant from
the local arts cooperative in the cramped back bedroom of an
ex-communist apartment block in Tbilisi or Kutaisi

but at the time of writing your biographical details are
extremely hazy;

however, I feel sure that by the time this poem sees the light
of day *Wire* magazine will have honoured you with a far more
extensive profile than you last merited when mention of that
wonderful Pharrell remix

was sandwiched between longer pieces on the notorious
Kyoto-based noise guitarist Idiot O'Clock, and a woman
called Sonic Pleasure who plays the housebricks.

However this little I have gleaned: firstly, that you are
married to Thomas Brinkmann, whose records are boring –
an opinion I held long before love carried me away –

and, secondly, that TBA

is not an acronym, as I had first assumed, but Georgian for
'lake' – in which case it probably has a silent 't', like 'Tbilisi',
and so is pronounced *baa*

which serendipitously rhymes a bit with my only other word
of Georgian, being your term for 'mother' which is 'dada', or
possibly 'father' which is 'mama'.

I doubt we will ever meet, unless this somehow reaches you
on the wind;

we will never sit with a glass of tea in your local wood-lined
café while I close-question you on how you programmed that
unbelievably great snare on 'Wind',

of such brickwalled yet elastic snap it sounded exactly like a
12" plastic ruler bent back and released with great violence on
the soft gong

of a large white arse, if not one white for long.

But Natalie – Tusja, if I may – I will not pretend I hold much
hope for us, although I have, I confess, worked up my little
apologia:

I am not like those other middle-agey I-

DM enthusiasts: I have none of their hangdog pathos, my
geekery is the dirty secret that it should be

and what I lack in hair, muscle-tone and rugged good looks I
make up for with a dry and ready wit . . . but I know that time
and space conspire against me.

At least, my dear, let me wish you the specific best:
     may you be blessed
with the wonderful instrument you deserve, fitted – at the
time of writing – with a 2 GHz dual-core Intel chip and
enough double-pumped DDR2 RAM for the most CPU-
intensive processes;
     then no longer will all those gorgeous acoustic spaces

     be accessible only via an offline procedure involving a
freeware convolution reverb and an imperfectly recorded
impulse response of the Concertgebouw made illegally with a
hastily erected stereo pair and an exploded crisp bag
     for I would have all your plug-ins run in real-time, in the
blameless zero-latency heaven of the 32-bit floating-point
environment, with no buffer-glitch or freeze or dropout or lag;
     I would also grant you a golden midi controller, of such
responsiveness, smoothness of automation, travel and
increment
     that you would think it a transparent intercessor, a mere
copula, and feel machine and animal suddenly blent.

     This I wish you as I leave Inverkeithing and Fife
     listening to *Trepa N* for the two hundred and thirty-fourth
time in my life

with every hair on my right arm rising in non-fascistic one-armed salutation

towards Natalie, Tba, my Tusja, and all the mountain lakes of her small nation.

Rain

I love all films that start with rain:
rain, braiding a windowpane
or darkening a hung-out dress
or streaming down her upturned face;

one big thundering downpour
right through the empty script and score
before the act, before the blame,
before the lens pulls through the frame

to where the woman sits alone
beside a silent telephone
or the dress lies ruined on the grass
or the girl walks off the overpass,

and all things flow out from that source
along their fatal watercourse.
However bad or overlong
such a film can do no wrong,

so when his native twang shows through
or when the boom dips into view
or when her speech starts to betray
its adaptation from the play,

I think to when we opened cold
on a starlit gutter, running gold
with the neon of a drugstore sign
and I'd read into its blazing line:

forget the ink, the milk, the blood –
all was washed clean with the flood
we rose up from the falling waters
the falling rain's own sons and daughters

and none of this, none of this matters.

HERE

I must quit sleeping in the afternoon.
I do it for my heart, but all too soon
my heart has called it off. It does not love me.
If it downed tools, there'd soon be nothing of me.
Its hammer-beat says *you are*, not *I am*.
It prints me off here like a telegram.
What do *I* say? How can the lonely word
know who has sent it out, or who has heard?
Long years since I came round in her womb
enough myself to know I was not home,
my dear sea up in arms at the wrong shore
and her loud heart like a landlord at the door.
Where are we now? What misdemeanor sealed
my transfer? Mother, why so far afield?

THE BIG LISTENER

for Tony Blair

Midnight. Connaught Square. A headlight beam
finds Cherie just back from her speaking date.
She looks at you. Less animal of late.
You lose no sleep, but wake within a dream.
Your favourite: that old divided dark,
the white square at your neck; your good ear bent
towards the long sighs of your penitent.
You rinse a thousand souls before the lark
and wake refreshed, if somewhat at a loss
as to why they seem so lost for words.
They are your dead, who still rose to the birds
the day we filled the booths and made the cross,
before you'd forced them howling to their knees
to suffer your attentions. Spare us. Please.

WAVE

For months I'd moved across the open water
like a wheel under its skin, a frictionless
and by then almost wholly abstract matter
with nothing in my head beyond the bliss
of my own breaking, how the long foreshore
would hear my full confession, and I'd drain
into the shale till I was filtered pure.
There was no way to tell on that bare plain
but I felt my power run down with the miles
and by the time I saw the scattered sails,
the painted front and children on the pier
I was nothing but a fold in her blue gown
and knew I was already in the clear.
I hit the beach and swept away the town.

THE AIR

What is this dark and silent caravan
that being nowhere, neither comes nor goes;
that being never, has no hour or span;
of which we can say only that it flows?
How was it that this empty datastream,
this cache of dead light could so lose its way
it wandered back to feed on its own dream?
How did that dream grow to the waking day?
What is the sound that fades up from the hiss,
like a glass some random downdraught had set ringing,
now full of its only note, its lonely call,
drawing on its song to keep it singing?
When will the air stop breathing? Will it all
come to nothing, if nothing came to this?

MERCIES

She might have had months left of her dog-years,
but to be who? She'd grown light as a nest
and spent the whole day under her long ears
listening to the bad radio in her breast.
On the steel bench, knowing what was taking shape
she tried and tried to stand, as if to sign
that she was still of use, and should escape
our selection. So I turned her face to mine,
and seeing only love there – which, for all
the wolf in her, she knew as well as we did –
she lay back down and let the needle enter.
And love was surely what her eyes conceded
as her stare grew hard, and one bright aerial
quit making its report back to the centre.

THE ROUNDABOUT

for Jamie and Russ

It's moving still, that wooden roundabout
we found at the field's end, sunk in the grass
like an ancient buckler from the giants' war.
The first day of good weather, our first out
after me and your mother. Its thrawn mass
was like trying to push a tree over, or row
a galley sealed in ice. I was all for
giving up when we felt it give, and go.
What had saved the axle all those years?
It let out one great drawn-out yawn and swung
away like a hundred gates. Our hands still burning
we lay and looked up at a sky so clear
there was nothing in the world to prove our turning
but our light heads, and the wind's lung.

Nick Laird

Cuttings

Methodical dust shades the combs and pomade
while the wielded goodwill of the sunlight picks out
a patch of paisley wallpaper to expand leisurely on it.

The cape comes off with a matador's flourish
and the scalp's washed to get rid of the chaff.
This is the closeness casual once in the trenches

and is deft as remembering when not to mention
the troubles or women or prison.
They talk of the parking or calving or missing.

A beige lino, a red barber's chair, one ceramic brown sink
and a scenic wall-calendar of the glories of Ulster
sponsored by JB Crane Hire or some crowd flogging
    animal feed.

About, say, every second month or so
he will stroll and cross the widest street in Ireland
and step beneath the bandaged pole.

Eelmen, gunmen, the long dead, the police.
And my angry and beautiful father:
tilted, expectant and open as in a deckchair

outside on the drive, persuaded to wait
for a meteor shower, but with his eyes budded shut,
his head full of lather and unusual thoughts.

Poetry

It's a bit like looking through the big window
on the top deck of the number 47.

I'm watching you, and her, and all of them,
but through my own reflection.

Or opening my eyes when everyone's praying.
The wave machine of my father's breathing,

my mother's limestone-fingered steeple,
my sister's tiny fidgets, and me, moon-eyed, unforgetting.

And then the oak doors flapping slowly open to let us out,
like some great injured bird trying to take flight.

Pedigree

There are many of us.

My aunt,
the youngest sister,
is a reformed shoplifter.

An uncle breeds champion bantams.

Another, a pig-farmer,
has a racket smuggling cattle
back and forth and back across
the imaginary border.

Me, I've forty-seven cousins.

A scuffle over rustling sheep
became a stabbing in a bar outside Armagh,
and a murderer swings
from a branch high up in our family tree.

Which isn't a willow.

Instead,
an enormous unruly blackthorn hedge,

inside of which a corpse is tangled,
and sags from branch to branch,
like a dewy web:

a farmer jumped on the road, and strangled,
his pockets emptied
of the stock proceeds from the country fair
by two local Roman Catholic farmhands.

Riots in Donegal town when they were cleared.
And riots again when they were convicted.

I may be out on a limb.

One grandfather, the short-horn cattle dealer,
went bankrupt, calmly smoked his pipe,
and died at forty of lung cancer.

Martha, my grandmother, remade Heathhill a dairy farm
and when the rent man came
my mother'd hide behind the sofa with her brothers.

My father spent his boyhood fishing with a hook and tinfoil
    chocolate wrapper.

He coveted a Davy Crockett hat
and shined the medals of his legendary uncles
who'd all died at the Somme,
the Dragoon Guards of Inniskilling.

He left school without sitting his papers
and my mother dropped out to marry him.

Each evening after work and dinner,
she'd do her OU course,
and heave the brown suitcase of books
from out beneath the rickety, mythical bunks
I shared for ten years with my sister.

There is such a shelter in each other.

And you, you pad from the bathroom to Gershwin,
gentled with freckles and moisturized curves,
still dripping, made new, singing your footprints

as they singe the wood floor,
perfect in grammar and posture.

But before you passed me the phone
you were talking, and I couldn't help but note your tone,
as if you couldn't hear them right,
as if they were maybe calling
not just from across the water
but Timbuktu, or from the moon . . .

At least you can hear me, my darling,
I'm speaking so softly and clearly,
and this is a charge not a pleading.

Light Pollution

You're the patron saint of elsewhere,
jet-lagged and drinking apple juice,
eyeing, from the sixth-floor window,
a kidney-shaped swimming pool
the very shade of Hockney blue.

I know the left-hand view of life,
I think, and it's as if I have, of late,
forgotten something in the night –
I wake alone and freezing,
still keeping to my side.

Each evening tidal night rolls in
and the atmosphere is granted
a depth of field by satellites,
the hammock moon, aircraft
sinking into Heathrow.

Above the light pollution,
among the drift of stars tonight
there might be other traffic –
migrations of heron and crane,
their spectral skeins convergent

symbols, arrows, weather systems,
white flotillas bearing steadily
towards their summer feeding.
A million flapping sheets!
Who knows how they know?

The aids to navigation might be
memory and landmarks,

or the brightest constellations.
Perhaps some iron in the blood
detects magnetic north.

I wish one carried you some token,
some Post-it note or ticket,
some particular to document
this instant of self-pity –
His Orphic Loneliness, with Dog.

Advances? None miraculous,
though the deadness of the house
will mean your coming home
may seem an anti-climax
somehow, and a trespass.

Pug

Bruiser, batface, baby bear,
bounce in your moon suit
of apricot fur with some fluff
in your mouth or a twig or a feather.

Emperors bored you.

You with the prize-winning ears,
who grew from a glove
to a moccasin slipper
and have taken to secrecy

recently, worming in
under the furniture.
To discover you here
is to keep still and listen.

The settee begins wheezing.

*

Hogarth loved the fact
that for your first half-year
you hardly differed from a rabbit.
When you're over-excited

you tend to get hiccups.

You squeak when you yawn
and your tongue is unfurled
in a semi-circle, salmon-pink
on coastal rock, that trilobite

embedded in the slate
roof of your open mouth,
perfect for the mascot
of the House of Orange.

Your weapon of choice is the sneeze.

*

Above the winter garden
a hair-thin moon, reflecting.
You are open as a haiku,
all *karumi*, hint and sigh.

The Buddha would've liked you.

Watch us from your separate dream
then pad across to clamber through
the plastic flap and plant your paws
four-square again on grass, like this.

Your hackles bristle and you ridge
your back and bark and bark and bark,
at shadows and the fence,
at everything behind the fence,

the cuttings and the railway foxes.

Lipstick

Like nowhere on God's earth, this nightmare
we'd fought all year to liberate, and then
couldn't rouse the sleepers from. How could there

be an adequate description
of that camp, that passage of our lives,
the abject horror in which my men

and I arrived in April 1945.
The place was picked clean as a chicken run,
and everywhere were corpses: some in piles,

some alone or still in pairs, wherever they had fallen.
I fear it was some time before
one could grow accustomed to the sight of men

literally collapsing as one neared,
and could stop oneself assisting.
One had to get one's mind trained to the idea

that an individual did not count. That was the thing:
one knew five hundred souls a day were dying
and that five hundred souls a day were going

to go on falling dead for weeks, before anything
that we could do would have the least effect.
But it wasn't easy watching, say, a child choking

from diphtheria when one could guess
that an instant tracheotomy
would probably have saved her. Scores were left

to choke and drown in their own vomit,
because they lacked the strength to turn aside
and clear a passage for it.

And also dysentery, they squatted
out like animals, relieved themselves in the open.
I saw a woman washing once, naked,

with some general-issue soap and
watched her taking water from a cistern
in which a baby's body floated.

It was hopeless. The Red Cross came, its British
arm, and shortly after – it might not be connected –
there appeared, from somewhere, boxes of it: lipstick.

This was not what we wanted at all. We were calling for a hundred,
a thousand other things. I was embarrassed, then enraged.
Who had requested this – its name was printed

on the shipment – *Everlasting Rouge*?
Would you believe they thought it was the action of a genius?
The internees, when the news

(as it always did) got out, began beseeching
us for *lippenstift, der lippenstift*. For me at least
it was the darkest ring of something, seeing

how those women lay with no nightdress or sheets
but still that redness on their lips. I saw them
wandering, vampiric, red flecks on their teeth,

or sat alone, clown-like and lost. Awaiting post mortem,
lipstick in her clutch, I remember one dead on a table . . .
Dispatched to England in the autumn

I found my wife's cosmetics, wrapped them in a parcel
and flung it in a tip; though I still see that shade at times,
on hoardings or the high road, young mums, some skinny girl

who's coloured in the colour of her screams.

from The Art of War

WAGING WAR

This evening at dinner your very existence
was enough to disprove Darwin.
I outhitlered Hitler.

These nightly show-trials are
becoming tiresome and fractious,
each decree absolute and absurdly revanchist.

You swear that it's me who's obsessed with war,
the sting of a nettle, a national recession,
monsoons and ice avalanches,

and any particular
type of fucking depression
that I might, even now, dare to mention.

OFFENSIVE STRATEGY

Lately the tablets are making no difference.
I have started to cry during adverts again,
and dogs in particular set me off like a drain.

When I get into a fight queueing for petrol
you lie to your friends to account for my temper
and make me ring up for another appointment.

You want me to get a second opinion,
though you put it all down to my father,
just as my mother puts it all down to his.

Another way I can tell it is all going wrong
is I can't get enough nicotine in my system
and nothing will force me to speak.

I run for an hour and still can't get to sleep.
I seem to spend most of my time starting books
and then putting them back on the shelf.

Also, since punching the wall of the study
last Thursday I've been waking each dawn
with a fatter man's hand at the end of my wrist.

It is swollen and red and doesn't quite bend
while my fingers are stiff and insist on remaining
gestured away from the body, as if in disgust.

TERRAIN

Though we cannot detect them, infra-red rays from the system's
security sensors are scanning the rooms, and our surnames
are secret and neat in security ink on the back of the picture frames,

though readily fluorescent under ultraviolet light. In our own rainbow
of visibility, you'd been watching a property show and had dozed,
and now the screen was frantic, driving home through snow, alone.

I read somewhere one-hundredth of that static is cosmic radiation,
interfering from the very edge of space and time, some ninety billion
trillion miles away, from the word go, from the Big Bang.

Proponents of string theory posit twenty-six dimensions,
though we have the ability to pick up only four, with these senses
I can now detune – settled in beside your skin and warmth and sleep –

to some unnumbered octave, some unremembered reach,
where all the other universes press like lovers up against us.

MANOEUVRING

Manoeuvre, of course, from the Gaelic,
man meaning animal, and *oeuvre* meaning works,
thus *the workings of the beast* –

I heard the bomb at Teebane in which a friend died
and in Brixton once, fucking someone else,
a car backfired unexpectedly and I began to sob.

I couldn't stop. Reader, I almost married *her.*
Soldiers used to whisper beneath my bedroom window
and from the good room once I watched a murderer

get chased across the field below the fence,
and saw him punch and swear
and chew the ear off a detective sergeant.

That policeman sat two pews in front
in Derryloran church and knew I stared.
I couldn't stop. You are banging the door

and shouting about leaving.
Someone somewhere told me something,
that kindness is the thing.

Santa Maddalena

Cool air massing on the mountain
passes through the ruled bamboo
with rumours of Etruscan archers
underneath our open window,
drawing arrows, creaking bows.

We are each other's provocation
and since noon no one has spoken.
Even to myself I seem like something
withstood, but it will be dark in ten,

and I'm glad the linden by the pool
yields in the breeze, then steadies,
ordering the tremor of its leaves
again to an unbroken canopy,
like the shields of legionaries.

Women in Antiquity

At the checkout Cleopatra.
Eyelash. Nailtap.
The Queen of Sheba leaving Tie Rack.

Boadicea clipping tickets.
Three Venuses of Willendorf
blocking the exhibit.

Is each of these figurines
meant to represent the goddess?
Or constitute an offering from votaries

by way of worship? You express
surprise at such a wide variety,
and I stay absolutely silent.

Each wood or stone statue stands
and holds her breasts or clasps
her hands above her solar plexus,

and though the guide itemizes reasons
against nakedness: social; shame;
the cold; aesthetic; to turn aside

the evil eye; the first four are
discarded easily enough in argument,
I think, but the eye is mine.

Annals of Alan

My carrel on the eighth floor of lower Manhattan has a lot
of graffiti devoted to Alan. **Alan has the best weed.**
Alan is a woman. The walrus is Alan. Do we still need Alan?
Alan I want to have your baby. Alan taped my nana.
Fuck Obama Alan for president.

Alan is Geraldo Rivera. The victory is Alan's.
I hate being Alan. Alan is a dream most likely.
Who the heck is Alan? Alan is homosexy.
Alan is a social construct. *I love Alan.*
It all comes down to Alan. I AM ALAN.

Alan is over. We are all Alan. Remember when
there was no Alan? If I am so beautiful and if you love me so
much then spell my fucking name correctly –
ALLEN. No, it's Allan. No, it's Alain.
Alain, Alain, t'es beau et je t'aime.

Go Giants

Go go gadget legs. Go right. Go left.
Go wrong. Go west. Go down to the sea
in ships. Go down to the river and pray.
Go fish. Go first. Go forth and multiply.
Go in now and say goodbye. Go blind.
Go deaf. Go short. Go long. Go to press.

Go to pot. Go fuck yourself. Go straight.
Go Braves. Go jump in a lake. Go hard.
Go hide. Go down with a case of.
Go ape. Go without. Go Patriots.
Go halves. Go slow. Go under the knife.
Go under the sign of the war-shaft.

Go one better. Go great guns.
Go south. Go out in the midday sun.
Go red. Go blond. Go Vandals.
Go tell it on the mountain. Go and sin
no more. Go compare. Go nuclear.
Go back to E7 from E8. Go paperless.

Go Cowboys. Go Redskins. Go naked.
Go to ground. Go ahead. Go abroad.
Go to grass. Go slack. Go all ironic.
Go down in a blaze of. Go Titans.
Go for the sake of. Go Saints.
Go fly a kite. Go against. Go gaga.

Go in peace to love and serve the.
Go and get help. Go directly to jail.
Go down in flames. Go up in smoke.
Go for broke. Go tell Aunt Rhody.
Go tell the Spartans. Go to hell.
Go into detail. Go for the throat.

Talking in Kitchens

Our friend Michael comes by and we sit at the table,
eating a curry from the Bombay Bicycle Club
and passing the baby between us.

When Michael has left we head upstairs
and the baby's asleep and we've talked ourselves out
and we feel as we feel every day of the year

like nobody knows how we feel and it's fine,
because our secrets live near the secrets of others,
and our wants are not so mean.

Easement comes in the weirdest of places
like that blue fire lit in the wood-burning stove
or the face on the dog when she chews at a carrot.

Here it is written down if I forget to say it –
my home is the temple made by your hands.

To the Woman at the United Airlines Check-in Desk at Newark

Shonique, I am in time, and I know your fight
is hard: the fight is hard for everyone alive
and all those bodies in Departures

are naked under clothes and scarred –
that granted, even deeper scratches welt
and heal in weeks though still they smart

on contact, and I never really cared
for the terms I struck with earth,
more total war than limited skirmish.

I seethe, Shonique; I drink; I smoke weed
and seek relief from mental anguish;
the peopled life, car horns sounding down

on Houston. All three kinds of knowledge
fox me: outer, inner, pure mathematics –
but I understand your relatives are dying also

and I know the days are slow, the years fast,
that these are facts, however surprising.
Like you, I think the worst is yet to come,

plus there's time lifting everything in sight,
Shonique, pocketing orchids and mothers,
the little white pebbledashed bungalows –

you in your small corner and me in mine.
Let me be clear and accommodative, more
water than ice; and raise my hands to show

I mean no harm, and that I'm stupid,
and malicious, and if I'm trying to be fearless
I know it gives me no right to act like this.

What's understood is I'll be filed beneath
The Pricks, and fair enough. Very seldom
do I note the world wears a single face

with endless variations, and even then,
Shonique, it tends to be a face like yours,
one particularly fine. Speaking of which,

your florescent orange lip-sticked lip
curls up at all of me with such distaste now
I sit down on my case at the rush of shame I feel:

and also love; and of course lust, hate, remorse.

from Progress

(City of Destruction)

One thing I don't get used to is looking up
and seeing nothing, the heavens as gaunt
as a blanket thrown over a birdcage but

last night, back home, whole galaxies festooned
a sky outside my room, a few fields
and a stream and a deep lane from O'Neill's

old bawn, and a mile outside the market town
whose industries are matching; manufacturing
cement and processing the animals to meat.

.   .   .   .   .   .

(Hill Difficulty)

Our mild and violent land of the giant
leylandii and four-bar bitumen fences.
Of porn mags stashed in blackthorn hedges.

The snout of a shotgun nuzzling out under
the valance as the eldest goes hoking for
presents from Santa beneath the bed.

Should Orestes just have been acquitted,
walked off scot-free? Not hard to get blood
from a stone if it's smashed in someone's face.

.   .   .   .   .   .

(Mr Skill)

All the cities of antiquity were walled
and minute observation saves us.
Galileo, plotting the trajectories

of four nomadic specks near Jupiter,
procured proof of a nature indisputable
That Not Everything Revolves Around You,

and this was the first disconnect between
the eye and fist, a new truth that soon
eclipsed the other facts that left you foxed

and slightly teary: funfair mirrors,
the central locking, a magnetic catch
on your mother's shiny leather purse.

(Christian's Deplorable Condition)

Say, 90% cement and 10% meat
when I moved to Rome at thirty
fairly hopeful, fairly certain I might

begin some sort of self-taught course in
Appreciating Beauty, on how not to view
it solely with incipient suspicion,

a Covenanter's eye to waste – in any case
I entered the belly of the beast:
a city under occupation where each

(Land of Vainglory)

same-but-different priest would watch –
the pappy white hands clasped over the crotch –
as the checkout girl packed up his stuff:

Prosecco, zucchini, carta igienica –
and each time I wanted to obstruct,
like a friendly but finally menacing drunk,

and stand too close and interrupt and recount
at length how Tycho Brahe made himself
a metal nose, tipped with gold, and kept

beneath his table Jepp, the dwarf he thought
clairvoyant, and let his pet elk get so plastered
over dinner it stumbled down the stairs

and died.   I was thinking this:
that the history of history is ridiculous,
that these specifics were sufficient.

.   .   .   .   .   .

(Mr Brisk)

A stranger arrives at night in the city
with something extraordinary under his cloak,
a leather pole that makes the most

distant bodies close. One could put one's eye
to the contraption, spy on washerwomen
spreading their apparel on the reeds to dry,

a button of horn on the torn shirt
of a steeplejack climbing the doge's palace.
He had to act fast and thought it out that night:

the shopping list, extant, reads: sheet glass,
an organ pipe, slippers for the boy, chickpeas,
artillery balls of variant size.

(Hill Lucre)

The Senate ascends the Campanile:
he'd worked the magnification up to ten
and could identify quite easily

which galleon it was threading the horizon
an hour or more from harbour – information
worth a purseful to the merchants

crowding the Rialto – and when he'd worked
up a few more mercantile triumphs,
Galileo trained his novel apparatus

on the night, and look, up close the moon
is not featureless and luminous
but scarred as a clean peach stone.

.   .   .   .   .   .

(Valley of Humiliation)

Because the problem with leaving home
is home follows, and by the time Tyrone
left, having exhausted his usefulness,

he had been baited to his beard and mocked,
the lands lost, his rights to hunt and fish lost . . .
Fake obeisance, real fear, such dissimulation:

all that saps the character, infects the will
and the greatest danger to the English
since the time of Silken Thomas dwindled

in the warm south; his sight began to go;
he slept with an unsheathed sword by his side
and drank too much, and remembered, and attended

to matters with great pride and a little shame,
drafting letters home, complaining and battling with
Lombard, plotting the Spanish Ambassador's visit:

and those of us left eventually annexed
the fort at Tullyhogue for hide-and-seek,
then menthol cigarettes and adolescent sex.

.   .   .   .   .   .

(Enchanted Ground)

The noise of the breeze in the leaves is enormous.
The sound is the sound of an ocean
you stand at the edge of, an Atlantic unseen

with the naked eye but which you can taste
in the saltiness faint on her neck, on her breasts:
and amid the clang of bucklers, a hundred

harps aflutter, the Great O'Neill was crowned
atop the hill of Ireland's Youth . . . You grin
and lie flat out, shaded, lit, assuaged, watching

sky and supple leaf-print, holding and defending
nothing but the unzipped and unstrapped pitch-
perfect one beside you humming something

by the Smiths and tracing lightly cursive
shapes with a finger on your inside wrist.
A dandelion seed slides along its rill of air

and rises and rises and passes from sight.
Home is only one depiction of reality
and there are others, yes, but this is mine.

I look out from two nail-holes six feet up.
Most of my skin is lacking nerve endings
and my hearing's worse than the dog's but –

(*Mr Implacable*)

as to how I might attest to *presence* –
that thing lit and extraordinary –
I would cite the not infrequent

visits of the dandelion seed, aloft, adrift,
proceeding, streeling above Paradise,
ten thousand houses of the saddest news

where the lion's tooth, unloosed, brings
the same sensations of translucency
I experienced a lot on Zoloft and vodka

or Zispin and whiskey
and in certain passages of Ammons
or Edmund Burke or Wallace Stevens.

.   .   .   .   .   .

(Chastised by a Shining One)

David, I am getting to it.
If you would give me just a minute.
An ability to pull the graceful pint and tend

a bar I owe to you, my useful skill,
and the one which saw me mostly liquid
through my college years and law school.

You had come back for a spell from Australia
to see Annie, your mother, who'd suffered a scare,
and even there, by that, showed me the ropes.

.   .   .   .   .   .

(Reliever)

I mean once more with feeling. I mean
Allegri composed it at the commission
of Pope Urban, who reserved it for use

in the Tenebrae service during Holy Week,
that 3 a.m. sequence when the candles
are extinguished in the Sistine Chapel

one by one, until a single drop of flame
remains – and it is a fine baroque example
of how successfully the choral template

might adjust itself to fit an elliptic
non-contiguous life, since it embodies
what it indicates, and so the unison is

queried repeatedly with descant:
four songsters counter five – one slow chant
builds and then, across the chancel, a slant account

occurs – and when those other voices enter
it is like water meeting water
which forces some new channel open in

the mind – silvers, slivers, shafts and ribbons,
countershafts and anabranch, rills and winterbourne –
and each discrete human voice uncaps

a separate grade of light so when the counter-
tenor rests for four beats on the top C
you fall slightly upwards and desire to be clean.

(Valley of the Shadow)

David, it's been twenty years
and I hardly remember your face.
Your tremendous hair I do remember,

a kind of feather-cut highlighted mullet,
and your taste for the shoe-string leather-thong
neckties favoured by Mexican cattlemen.

The clip-clop of your cowboy boots.
The fury all goes somewhere and I'm sorry
about this. You were always a bit

self-conscious – as I was, and as I am
starting in the bar, fourteen and withdrawn
and gangly, and you're patient enough

with changing the barrels and cleaning the lines.
You banged on about the outback's open
endless roads, the shimmering heat and the red light

and the absolutely empty desert,
but you were only travelling back from Omagh
with the others, dayshifting with a roofer.

Our windows pulsed once, twice, but didn't break.
You had the right firmness, could make a joke
and still say no, and had grown stout enough

to be thumped or hugged or roughhoused
by any drunk at the weddings we'd do –
that we did – but you couldn't handle this.

When I drove past the brass plaque the last time
I saw some
had defaced it with a marker pen again.

(Giant Despair)

After that sustained top C you're jittery
as a compass needle, until the plainsong
starts again and the choruses are calling

forth responses from the other side:
the singing has the force of argument,
though since the final verse is sung by

(Man in an Iron Cage)

both choirs in harmony, an argument
concluding in something shared and singular,
like sleep or being human, subject

to that death – and why coax us in like that God?
Why the bait, the switch, the ambuscade?
(From the Latin, *to place in a wood*.)

Writing it down or performing it elsewhere
meant excommunication: this is dream
logic. In mine, a family gathering.

I mean the family plot. I mean two down
from Allingham at St Anne's in Ballyshannon.
Mise Eire. Meh! Deuce.

.   .   .   .   .   .

(Wicket Gate)

That lunchtime Fergus ate my sandwiches
and left my Mid-Ulster Mail torn up in
little printed petals on the wood-grain

of the melamine table. The canteen
fell silent when I came in and sat down
and looked up and did nothing.

(Gaius's Inn)

David, it's 3 a.m. and I am done.
I've turned all the bottles outwards
in the fridge below the till and you are

crossing the deserted parquet dance floor,
boot heels tapping, carrying a dustpan,
in the other hand a stacking chair –

(The Arbour)

I should say there is this density to objects,
and that they gather weight in time and spin
on without effort in their orbits gaining

traction, gravity and drag, a fullness in the
sense of things, and always drawing other
objects closer with a pull that lifts the whole

of you and sees you in safe and sound at home to
die a good death with family round you.
Fallacious, that, and what powers live on through us,

ordering their preferments and our lies,
do not give two fucks for us. We do as we are told.
The stars are hard and deaf and cold;

the river unconcerned about our presence
or its absence, and to paraphrase the meaning
is depletion of that meaning: even a one-to-one

map would lack both depth and texture: nicknames,
the favourite chocolate in the box of Roses,
how someone dries herself or dresses

after the shower, slowly, piece by piece,
wandering the flat on the phone to her sister,
all life's boring secret lovely histories,

minutiae of the dying who simply go on
dying now forever, the fixed blur of a spun
thing which spins so fast the focus of the eye

(Mr Honest)

cannot alight on it, can't print an image
on the retina but is repeatedly flung
off and forced by motion into motion.

Imagine how he sets the spared artillery ball
at the centre of the wheel to grind the lens,
how he pedals and then delicately leans

sheet glass into the metal surface so it shrieks
and sparks glitter out and he waits and then leans
the changed sheet of glass away . . .

(House Beautiful)

What if you felt nothing more walking down
the streets of Cookstown than you ever felt
walking in New York or Rome or London,

that you knew no one and the plenitude
of faces meant an openness and soft regard
for all the local gods, some dulling into love

by constant movement, children, music, dogs,
by the caramel or black or light pink
skin the people move and keep on moving

the miraculous flesh of their bodies in.

Feel Free

To deal with all the sensational loss I like to interface
with Earth. I like to do this in a number of ways.
I like to feel the work I am exerting being changed,

the weight of my person refigured, and I like to hang
above the ground, thus; hammocks, snorkeling, alcohol.
I also like the mind to feel a kind of neutral buoyancy

and to that end I set aside a day a week, Shabbat,
to not act. Having ceded independence to the sunset
I will not be shaving, illuminating rooms, or raising

the temperature of food. If occasionally I like to feel
the leavening of being near a much larger unnatural
tension, I walk off a Sunday through the high fields

of blanket bog, saxifrage, a few thin Belted Galloways,
rounding Lough Mallon to stand by the form of beauty
upheld in a scrubby acre at Creggandevsky, where I do

duck and enter under a capstone mapped by rival empires
of yellow feather-moss and powdery white lichen. I like
then to stop, crouched, and press my back on a housing

of actual rock, coldness which lives for a while on the skin.
And I like when I give you the nightfeed, Harvey, how you're
really concentrating on it: fists clenched, eyes shut, like *this*
   is bliss.

II

I like a steady disruption. I like it when the solid mantle turns
to shingle and water rushes up it over and over, in love.
My white-noise machine from Argos is set to Crashing Wave

but I'm not averse to the presence of numerous and minute
quanta moving very fast in unison; occasions when a light
wind undulates the ears of wheat, or a hessian sack of pearl-

barley seed is sliced with a pocket knife and pours. I like
the way it sounds pattering on stone. I like how the starlings
over Monti cohere and separate their bodies into one cyclonic

symphony, and I like that the hawk of the mind catches at
their purse, pulse, caul, arc. I like the excitation passing as
a shadow-ripple back and how the bag is snatched, rolls

slack; straight, falciform; mouthing; bulbing; a pumping
heart. I like to interface with millions of colored pixels
depicting attractive people procreating on a screen itself

dependent on rare metals mined by mud-gray children
who trudge up bamboo scaffolding above a grayish-red lake
of belching mud. I like how the furnace burning earth instills

in me reflexive gestures of timidity and self-pity and deference
as I walk along the kinder surfaces, grass, say, or sand,
unable ever to meet with my eyes the gaze of the sun.

III

I can imagine that my first and fifth marriages will be
to the same human, a woman, the first marriage working
well enough that we decide to try again as soon as it's,

you know, mutually convenient. I can see that. I like the fact
that we're 'supercooled star matter,' even if I can't envisage you
as anything other than warm and bleating. The thing is

I can be persuaded fairly easily to initiate immune responses
by the fake safety signals of national anthems, cleavage, family
photographs, country lanes, large-eyed mammals, fireworks,

the King James Bible, Nina Simone singing 'The Twelfth of Never,'
cave paintings, coffins, dolphins, dolmens. But I like it also
when the fat impasto of the canvas gets slashed by a tourist

with a claw hammer, and a glimpse is caught of what you couldn't
say. Entanglement I like, spooky action at a distance analogizing
some little thing including this long glance across the escalators

or how you know the song before you switch the station on.
When a photon of light meets a half-silvered mirror and splits
one meets the superposition of two, being twinned: and this repeats.

Tickling your back, Katherine, to get you to sleep, I like to lie here
with my eyes closed and think of my schoolfriends' houses, before
choosing one to walk through slowly, room by sunlit room.

ACKNOWLEDGEMENTS

For material included in this selection the following grateful acknowledgements are made: to Bloodaxe for poems by Kathleen Jamie from *Mr and Mrs Scotland are Dead: Poems 1980–1994* (2002); to Picador for poems by Kathleen Jamie from *Jizzen* (1999), *The Tree House* (2004), *The Overhaul* (2012) and *The Bonniest Companie* (2015); to Faber & Faber for poems by Don Paterson from *Orpheus: A Version of Rainer Marie Rilke* (2006), *Selected Poems* (2012) and *40 Sonnets* (2015); and to Faber & Faber for poems by Nick Laird from *To a Fault* (2005), *On Purpose* (2007) and *Go Giants* (2013).

'Feel Free' by Nick Laird first appeared in *The New Yorker*.